C000263523

SONGS FROM
HEAVEN AND EARTH
Selections from the Psalms with prayer meditations

©Copyright Scandinavia Publishing House
Nørregade 32
DK 1165 Copenhagen K
Denmark
Tel. 01-140091

© Text: Marlee Alex

Quotations from *the Holy Bible, International Version*,
copyright New York International Bible Society. Used by permission.

Printed in Hong Kong by C & C Offset Printing Co., Ltd.

ISBN 87 87732 87 4

SONGS FROM
HEAVEN AND EARTH

Selections from the Psalms with prayer meditations

Scripture text from The Holy Bible, New International Version

Text by Marlee Alex
Edited by Jørgen Vium Olesen

Scandinavia

Let the heavens
rejoice, let the earth
be glad; let the sea resound,
and all that is in it.

*Before the mountains
were born or you brought forth
the earth and the world, from
everlasting to everlasting
You are God.*

All My Fountains Are in Yo

He has set his foundation on the holy mountain.
As they make music they will sing, "All my fountains are in
you."

He has set his foundation on the holy mountain; the Lord
loves the gates of Zion more than all the dwellings of Jacob.
Glorious things are said of you, O city of God: *Selah*
"I will record Rahab and Babylon among those who
acknowledge me— Philistia too, and Tyre, along with Cush—
and will say, 'This one was born in Zion.' "
Indeed, of Zion it will be said, "This one and that one were
born in her, and the Most High himself will establish her."
The Lord will write in the register of the peoples: "This one
was born in Zion." *Selah*
As they make music they will sing, "All my fountains are in
you."

All my sources of refreshment are found in
you, city of God. You are the foundation of
life, and everything that makes it
meaningful for me. How privileged it is to
be born of the Spirit from above, to be born
in Zion.

I Cry Before You

You have overwhelmed me with all your waves. Selah

O Lord, the God who saves me, day and night I cry out before you.
May my prayer come before you; turn your ear to my cry.

For my soul is full of trouble and my life draws near the grave.
I am counted among those who go down to the pit; I am like a man without strength.
I am set apart with the dead, like the slain who lie in the grave, whom you remember no more, who are cut off from your care.

You have put me in the lowest pit, in the darkest depths.
Your wrath lies heavily upon me; you have overwhelmed me with all your waves. *Selah*
You have taken from me my closest friends and have made me repulsive to them.
I am confined and cannot escape; my eyes are dim with grief.

I call to you, O Lord, every day; I spread out my hands to you.
Do you show your wonders to the dead? Do those who are dead rise up and praise you? *Selah*
Is your love declared in the grave, your faithfulness in Destruction?
Are your wonders known in the place of darkness, or your righteous deeds in the land of oblivion?
But I cry to you for help, O Lord; in the morning my prayer comes before you.
Why, O Lord, do you reject me and hide your face from me?
From my youth I have been afflicted and close to death; I have suffered your terrors and am in despair.
Your wrath has swept over me; your terrors have destroyed me.
All day long they surround me like a flood; they have completely engulfed me.
You have taken my companions and loved ones from me; the darkness is my closest friend.

When things are darkest Lord, it is the darkness of Your shadow hovering over me, reminding me You are very close. I cling to that knowledge, embracing it as my dearest companion.

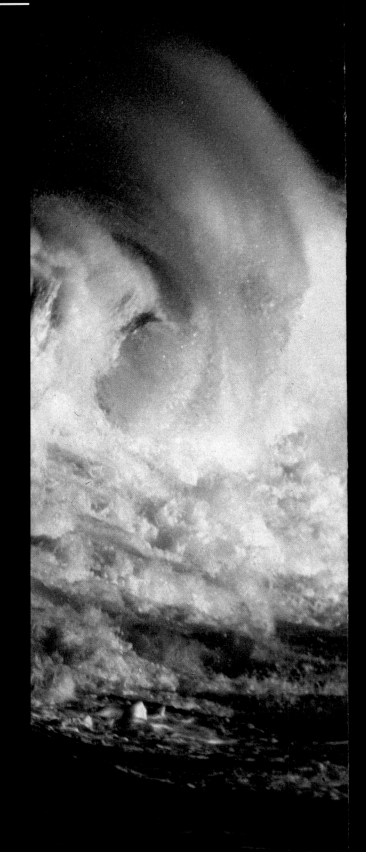

O Lord Almighty, Who Is Like You?

I will sing of the Lord's great love forever; with my mouth I will make your faithfulness known through all generations. I will declare that your love stands firm forever, that you established your faithfulness in heaven itself.

You said, "I have made a covenant with my chosen one, I have sworn to David my servant, 'I will establish your line forever and make your throne firm through all generations.' "
Selah

The heavens praise your wonders, O Lord, your faithfulness too, in the assembly of the holy ones.
For who in the skies above can compare with the Lord? Who is like the Lord among the heavenly beings?
In the council of the holy ones God is greatly feared; he is more awesome than all who surround him.
O Lord God Almighty, who is like you? You are mighty, O Lord, and your faithfulness surrounds you.

You rule over the surging sea; when its waves mount up, you still them.
You crushed Rahab like one of the slain; with your strong arm you scattered your enemies.
The heavens are yours, and yours also the earth; you founded the world and all that is in it.
You created the north and the south; Tabor and Hermon sing for joy at your name.
Your arm is endued with power; your hand is strong, your right hand exalted.

Righteousness and justice are the foundation of your throne; love and faithfulness go before you.
Blessed are those who have learned to acclaim you, who walk in the light of your presence, O Lord.
They rejoice in your name all day long; they exult in your righteousness.
For you are their glory and strength, and by your favor you exalt our horn.
Indeed, our shield belongs to the Lord, our king to the Holy One of Israel.

I will join the skies and seas, Lord, in verbalizing the faithfulness of Your love. My poor words do not serve me well. I seek accompaniment by the clouds, the waves, the mountains, and the lights of the sky. We will together acclaim Your faithfulness and rejoice in Your love.

Will Maintain My
indness to Him Forever

set his hand over the sea, his right hand over the rivers.

you spoke in a vision, to your faithful people you said:
ve bestowed strength on a warrior; I have exalted a
g man from among the people.
e found David my servant; with my sacred oil I have
ted him.
and will sustain him; surely my arm will strengthen him.
emy will subject him to tribute; no wicked man will
ss him.
crush his foes before him and strike down his
saries.
ithful love will be with him, and through my name his
will be exalted.
set his hand over the sea, his right hand over the rivers.
ll call out to me, 'You are my Father, my God, the Rock
vior.'
also appoint him my firstborn, the most exalted of the
of the earth.
maintain my love to him forever, and my covenant with
ill never fail.
establish his line forever, his throne as long as the
ns endure.
s sons forsake my law and do not follow my statutes, if
violate my decrees and fail to keep my commands, I will
n their sin with the rod, their iniquity with flogging; but I
ot take my love from him, nor will I ever betray my
ulness.
not violate my covenant or alter what my lips have
d.
for all, I have sworn by my holiness– and I will not lie to
– that his line will continue forever and his throne
e before me like the sun; it will be established forever
e moon, the faithful witness in the sky." *Selah*

ne things, Lord, You have established
rnally. It is marvellous to contemplate
y few, and how simple these things are.
ny need, I am reduced to the memory of
ur love and faithfulness and the hope of
eriencing it again.

God Hides Himself; But Not Forever

How long, O Lord? Will you hide yourself forever?

But you have rejected, you have spurned, you have been very angry with your anointed one.
You have renounced the covenant with your servant and have defiled his crown in the dust.
You have broken through all his walls and reduced his strongholds to ruins.
All who pass by have plundered him; he has become the scorn of his neighbors.
You have exalted the right hand of his foes; you have made all his enemies rejoice.
You have turned back the edge of his sword and have not supported him in battle.
You have put an end to his splendor and cast his throne to the ground.
You have cut short the days of his youth; you have covered him with a mantle of shame. *Selah*

How long, O Lord? Will you hide yourself forever? How long will your wrath burn like fire?
Remember how fleeting is my life. For what futility you have created all men!
What man can live and not see death, or save himself from the power of the grave? *Selah*
O Lord, where is your former great love, which in your faithfulness you swore to David?
Remember, Lord, how your servant has been mocked, how I bear in my heart the taunts of all the nations, the taunts with which your enemies have mocked, O Lord, with which they have mocked every step of your anointed one.
Praise be to the Lord forever! Amen and Amen.

You've turned your back to me, Lord. I am broken. My life is futile, I am reduced to the mere memory of Your love. But in that memory You whisper. A time. A purpose. A step forward, not back.

Give Me A Heart of Wisdom

Before the mountains were born or you brought forth the earth and the world, from everlasting to everlasting you are God.

Lord, you have been our dwelling place throughout all generations.
Before the mountains were born or you brought forth the earth and the world, from everlasting to everlasting you are God.

You turn men back to dust, saying, "Return to dust, O sons of men."
For a thousand years in your sight are like a day that has just gone by, or like a watch in the night.
You sweep men away in the sleep of death; they are like the new grass of the morning– though in the morning it springs up new, by evening it is dry and withered.

We are consumed by your anger and terrified by your indignation.
You have set our iniquities before you, our secret sins in the light of your presence.
All our days pass away under your wrath; we finish our years with a moan.
The length of our days is seventy years– or eighty, if we have the strength; yet their span is but trouble and sorrow, for they quickly pass, and we fly away.

Who knows the power of your anger? For your wrath is as great as the fear that is due you.
Teach us to number our days aright, that we may gain a heart of wisdom.
Relent, O Lord! How long will it be? Have compassion on your servants.
Satisfy us in the morning with your unfailing love, that we may sing for joy and be glad all our days.
Make us glad for as many days as you have afflicted us, for as many years as we have seen trouble.

May your deeds be shown to your servants, your splendor to their children.
May the favor of the Lord our God rest upon us; establish the work of our hands for us– yes, establish the work of our hands.

My feelings and behavior are so unstable, Lord. The results of my efforts are inconsequential and futile. Only in You, do I sense a sweetness in the triviality of my days. I count on You; establish the work of my hands and make something eternal out of it.

The Lord Will Be My Dwelling

You will tread upon the lion and the cobra; you will trample the great lion and the serpent.

He who dwells in the shelter of the Most High will rest in the shadow of the Almighty.
I will say of the Lord, "He is my refuge and my fortress, my God, in whom I trust."

Surely he will save you from the fowler's snare and from the deadly pestilence.
He will cover you with his feathers, and under his wings you will find refuge; his faithfulness will be your shield and rampart.
You will not fear the terror of night, nor the arrow that flies by day, nor the pestilence that stalks in the darkness, nor the plague that destroys at midday.
A thousand may fall at your side, ten thousand at your right hand, but it will not come near you.
You will only observe with your eyes and see the punishment of the wicked.

If you make the Most High your dwelling– even the Lord, who is my refuge– then no harm will befall you, no disaster will come near your tent.
For he will command his angels concerning you to guard you in all your ways; they will lift you up in their hands, so that you will not strike your foot against a stone.
You will tread upon the lion and the cobra; you will trample the great lion and the serpent.

"Because he loves me," says the Lord, "I will rescue him; I will protect him, for he acknowledges my name.
He will call upon me, and I will answer him; I will be with him in trouble, I will deliver him and honor him.
With long life will I satisfy him and show him my salvation."

My spirit is only at home in you, Lord. And nothing can touch it, as long as I remain there. You have promised to be with me always, even to the end of the age. The dangers of this world needn't make me fear. I love being near You.

As they make
music they will sing,
"All my fountains
are in You".

24

Planted in the House of the Lord

The righteous will flourish like a palm tree, they will grow like a cedar of Lebanon; planted in the house of the Lord, they will flourish in the courts of our God.
They will still bear fruit in old age, they will stay fresh and green.

It is good to praise the Lord and make music to your name, O Most High, to proclaim your love in the morning and your faithfulness at night, to the music of the ten-stringed lyre and the melody of the harp.

For you make me glad by your deeds, O Lord; I sing for joy at the works of your hands.
How great are your works, O Lord, how profound your thoughts!
The senseless man does not know, fools do not understand, that though the wicked spring up like grass and all evildoers flourish, they will be forever destroyed.

But you, O Lord, are exalted forever.

For surely your enemies, O Lord, surely your enemies will perish; all evildoers will be scattered.
You have exalted my horn like that of a wild ox; fine oils have been poured upon me.
My eyes have seen the defeat of my adversaries; my ears have heard the rout of my wicked foes.

The righteous will flourish like a palm tree, they will grow like a cedar of Lebanon; planted in the house of the Lord, they will flourish in the courts of our God.
They will still bear fruit in old age, they will stay fresh and green, proclaiming, "The Lord is upright; he is my Rock, and there is no wickedness in him."

To be made fruitful God, sometimes seems so great a process. And yet, Your thoughts are deep. They take in many more perspectives than I've ever dreamed of. And so while I wait to grow and mature, I'll express what is natural for me now: The music Your love and goodness make me feel.

The Lord Reigns

The world is firmly established; it cannot be moved.
Mightier than the thunder of the great waters, mightier than
the breakers of the sea– the Lord on high is mighty.

The Lord reigns, he is robed in majesty; the Lord is robed in
majesty and is armed with strength.
The world is firmly established; it cannot be moved.
Your throne was established long ago; you are from all
eternity.

The seas have lifted up, O Lord, the seas have lifted up their
voice; the seas have lifted up their pounding waves.
Mightier than the thunder of the great waters, mightier than
the breakers of the sea– the Lord on high is mighty.

Your statutes stand firm; holiness adorns your house for
endless days, O Lord.

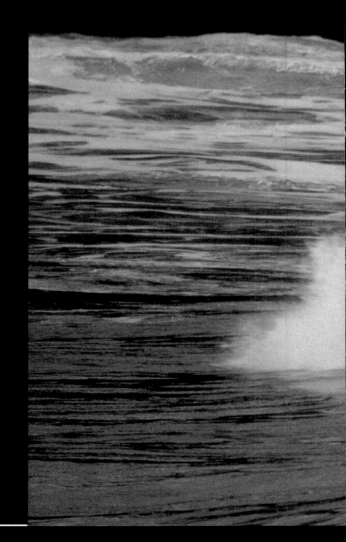

I love the atmosphere that antiques bring
into a home, somehow reflecting the
stability of old values. Your house is
decorated with holiness, Lord. Its
foundations are eternally old, and totally
stable. I am the temple of Your Holy Spirit.
Reign in me, so others sense the holiness of
Yourself.

O God Who Avenges, Shine Forth

Judgment will again be founded on righteousness, and all the upright in heart will follow it.

O Lord, the God who avenges, O God who avenges, shine forth.
Rise up, O Judge of the earth; pay back to the proud what they deserve.
How long will the wicked, O Lord, how long will the wicked be jubilant?

They pour out arrogant words; all the evildoers are full of boasting.
They crush your people, O Lord; they oppress your inheritance.
They slay the widow and the alien; they murder the fatherless.
They say, "The Lord does not see; the God of Jacob pays no heed."
Take heed, you senseless ones among the people; you fools, when will you become wise?
Does he who implanted the ear not hear? Does he who formed the eye not see?
Does he who disciplines nations not punish? Does he who teaches man lack knowledge?
The Lord knows the thoughts of man; he knows that they are futile.

Blessed is the man you discipline, O Lord, the man you teach from your law; you grant him relief from days of trouble, till a pit is dug for the wicked.
For the Lord will not reject his people; he will never forsake his inheritance.
Judgment will again be founded on righteousness, and all the upright in heart will follow it.

How many times have we pinned for Your help, and felt desperately forgotten? We are crushed by the plight of the persecuted people in our world. We who know You, long to make a difference. Exchange our futile thoughts for Yours, Lord. Discipline us to restore Your righteous judgment.

He Will Repay

When I said, "My foot is slipping,"your love, O Lord, supported me.

Who will rise up for me against the wicked? Who will take a stand for me against evildoers?
Unless the Lord had given me help, I would soon have dwelt in the silence of death.
When I said, "My foot is slipping," your love, O Lord, supported me.
When anxiety was great within me, your consolation brought joy to my soul.

Can a corrupt throne be allied with you—one that brings on misery by its decrees?
They band together against the righteous and condemn the innocent to death.
But the Lord has become my fortress, and my God the rock in whom I take refuge.
He will repay them for their sins and destroy them for their wickedness; the Lord our God will destroy them.

The joy of the Lord is my strength, the love of the Lord is my inspiration. I live with the daily newspaper in a world of corruption and decay. I need your presence fresh every day to light up my little corner of it.

Shout Aloud to the Rock

Come, let us bow down in worship, let us kneel before the Lord our Maker; for he is our God and we are the people of his pasture, the flock under his care.

Come, let us sing for joy to the Lord; let us shout aloud to the Rock of our salvation.
Let us come before him with thanksgiving and extol him with music and song.

For the Lord is the great God, the great King above all gods. In his hand are the depths of the earth, and the mountain peaks belong to him.
The sea is his, for he made it, and his hands formed the dry land.

Come, let us bow down in worship, let us kneel before the Lord our Maker; for he is our God and we are the people of his pasture, the flock under his care.

Today, if you hear his voice, do not harden your hearts as you did at Meribah, as you did that day at Massah in the desert, where your fathers tested and tried me, though they had seen what I did.
For forty years I was angry with that generation; I said, "They are a people whose hearts go astray, and they have not known my ways."
So I declared on oath in my anger, "They shall never enter my rest."

To know that I am one of Your flock, Lord, is one of the most precious treasures of my heart. And you have promised to give us Your kingdom. My heart is so vulnerable to outside influences. But it is soft toward You. Lead me to where You pasture Your flock, that I can enter into Your rest.

Worship the Lord

*Let the heavens rejoice, let the earth be glad; let the sea
resound, and all that is in it; let the fields be jubilant, and
everything in them.
Then all the trees of the forest will sing for joy; they will sing
before the Lord, for he comes, he comes to judge the earth.
He will judge the world in righteousness and the peoples in his
truth.*

Sing to the Lord a new song; sing to the Lord, all the earth.
Sing to the Lord, praise his name; proclaim his salvation day
after day.
Declare his glory among the nations, his marvelous deeds
among all peoples.

For great is the Lord and most worthy of praise; he is to be
feared above all gods.
For all the gods of the nations are idols, but the Lord made the
heavens.
Splendor and majesty are before him; strength and glory are
in his sanctuary.

Ascribe to the Lord, O families of nations, ascribe to the Lord
glory and strength.
Ascribe to the Lord the glory due his name; bring an offering
and come into his courts.
Worship the Lord in the splendor of his holiness; tremble
before him, all the earth.

Say among the nations, "The Lord reigns."
The world is firmly established, it cannot be moved; he will
judge the peoples with equity.
Let the heavens rejoice, let the earth be glad; let the sea
resound, and all that is in it; let the fields be jubilant, and
everything in them.
Then all the trees of the forest will sing for joy; they will sing
before the Lord, for he comes, he comes to judge the earth. He
will judge the world in righteousness and the peoples in his
truth.

*If the trees can rejoice as they anticipate
Your coming; then I can also, Lord. And I
will. I will be hopeful in my world because I
know Your character. I won't be outdone in
joy by the seas and the fields... You are not
only my creator but my savior as well.*

Light Is Shed

Let the earth be glad; let the distant shores rejoice.

Clouds and thick darkness surround him; righteousness and justice are the foundation of his throne.
His lightning lights up the world; the earth sees and trembles.
The mountains melt like wax before the Lord, before the Lord of all the earth.
The heavens proclaim his righteousness, and all the peoples see his glory.

The Lord reigns, let the earth be glad; let the distant shores rejoice.

Clouds and thick darkness surround him; righteousness and justice are the foundation of his throne.
Fire goes before him and consumes his foes on every side.
His lightning lights up the world; the earth sees and trembles.
The mountains melt like wax before the Lord, before the Lord of all the earth.
The heavens proclaim his righteousness, and all the peoples see his glory.

All who worship images are put to shame, those who boast in idols– worship him, all you gods!

Zion hears and rejoices and the villages of Judah are glad because of your judgments, O Lord.
For you, O Lord, are the Most High over all the earth; you are exalted far above all gods.

Let those who love the Lord hate evil, for he guards the lives of his faithful ones and delivers them from the hand of the wicked.
Light is shed upon the righteous and joy on the upright in heart.
Rejoice in the Lord, you who are righteous, and praise his holy name.

Light is shed from Your rainbow of promises, God. And each of Your promises is more radiant than the one before. Joy falls, sometimes like rain across our perspectives of sorrow, softening the hard soil of pain. We see a revelation of the unexpectedly glorious ingredients of ordinary light, of ordinary existence. We see the colors of Your love.

The heavens are
yours, and yours also
the earth; you founded
the world and all
that is in it.

He Has Remembered His Love

Let the sea resound, and everything in it, the world, and all who live in it.
Let the rivers clap their hands, let the mountains sing together for joy; let them sing before the Lord, for he comes to judge the earth.

Sing to the Lord a new song, for he has done marvelous things; his right hand and his holy arm have worked salvation for him.
The Lord has made his salvation known and revealed his righteousness to the nations.
He has remembered his love and his faithfulness to the house of Israel; all the ends of the earth have seen the salvation of our God.

Shout for joy to the Lord, all the earth, burst into jubilant song with music; make music to the Lord with the harp, with the harp and the sound of singing, with trumpets and the blast of the ram's horn– shout for joy before the Lord, the King.

Let the sea resound, and everything in it, the world, and all who live in it.
Let the rivers clap their hands, let the mountains sing together for joy; let them sing before the Lord, for he comes to judge the earth. He will judge the world in righteousness and the peoples with equity.

Nature is noisy in its song to You. Why should I be timid and trite? I want to be as creative in praising, as You were in creating the world. I'll find a new way to sing You a new song, Lord!

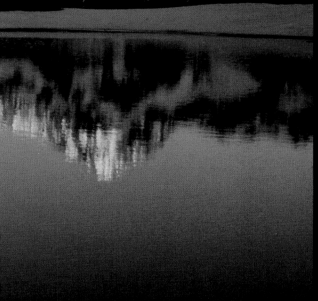

He Loves Justice

Exalt the Lord our God and worship at his holy mountain, for the Lord our God is holy.

The Lord reigns, let the nations tremble; he sits enthroned between the cherubim, let the earth shake.
Great is the Lord in Zion; he is exalted over all the nations.
Let them praise your great and awesome name– he is holy.

The King is mighty, he loves justice– you have established equity; in Jacob you have done what is just and right.
Exalt the Lord our God and worship at his footstool; he is holy.

Moses and Aaron were among his priests, Samuel was among those who called on his name; they called on the Lord and he answered them.
He spoke to them from the pillar of cloud; they kept his statutes and the decrees he gave them.

O Lord our God, you answered them; you were to Israel a forgiving God, though you punished their misdeeds.
Exalt the Lord our God and worship at his holy mountain, for the Lord our God is holy.

You are in control. You are in control of the nations and the universe. But when we call on You, You are personal. You affect our human destinies as individuals. I want to live life on a higher plane than I have until now. Draw me closer to Your holiness.

We Are His

It is he who made us, and we are his; we are his people, the sheep of his pasture.

Shout for joy to the Lord, all the earth.
Serve the Lord with gladness; come before him with joyful songs.
Know that the Lord is God. It is he who made us, and we are his; we are his people, the sheep of his pasture.

Enter his gates with thanksgiving and his courts with praise; give thanks to him and praise his name.
For the Lord is good and his love endures forever; his faithfulness continues through all generations.

I find my security, Lord, in knowing that it isn't I who have chosen You, but it is You who have chosen me. You created me and You bought me for Yourself with the blood of Christ. Thank you, Father.

The Faithful in the Land

My eyes will be on the faithful in the land, that they may dwell with me; he whose walk is blameless will minister to me.

I will sing of your love and justice; to you, O Lord, I will sing praise.
I will be careful to lead a blameless life– when will you come to me?

I will walk in my house with blameless heart.
I will set before my eyes no vile thing.

The deeds of faithless men I hate; they will not cling to me.
Men of perverse heart shall be far from me; I will have nothing to do with evil.

Whoever slanders his neighbor in secret, him will I put to silence; whoever has haughty eyes and a proud heart, him will I not endure.
My eyes will be on the faithful in the land, that they may dwell with me; he whose walk is blameless will minister to me.

No one who practices deceit will dwell in my house; no one who speaks falsely will stand in my presence.

Every morning I will put to silence all the wicked in the land; I will cut off every evildoer from the city of the Lord.

To be perfect, Father, as You are perfect is a mighty high calling. The thought of it nearly devastates me before I even start out. There is only one way to be sure I can reach those heights. Every morning will find me sitting quietly and listening at the feet of Jesus.

Answer Me Quickly

I lie awake; I have become like a bird alone on a housetop.

Hear my prayer, O Lord; let my cry for help come to you.
Do not hide your face from me when I am in distress. Turn
your ear to me; when I call, answer me quickly.

For my days vanish like smoke; my bones burn like glowing
embers.
My heart is blighted and withered like grass; I forget to eat my
food.
Because of my loud groaning I am reduced to skin and bones.
I am like a desert owl, like an owl among the ruins.
I lie awake; I have become like a bird alone on a housetop.
All day long my enemies taunt me; those who rail against me
use my name as a curse.
For I eat ashes as my food and mingle my drink with tears
because of your great wrath, for you have taken me up and
thrown me aside.
My days are like the evening shadow; I wither away like
grass.

*My small children don't like to see me sit or
lie with my eyes closed. They insist on
prying them open with grubby little fingers,
so my face is open to them. Your word says
you never slumber or sleep, Lord. Yet
sometimes I feel Your eyes closed to me.
And I want to look into them to understand
the whys of what You allow in my life.*

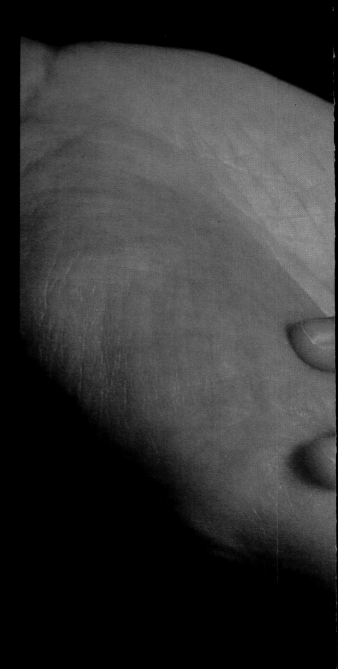

Written for a Future Generation

Let this be written for a future generation, that the people not yet created may praise the Lord:
"The Lord looked down from his sanctuary on high, from heaven he viewed the earth, to hear the groans of the prisoners and release those condemned to death."

But you, O Lord, sit enthroned forever; your renown endures through all generations.
You will arise and have compassion on Zion, for it is time to show favor to her; the appointed time has come.
For her stones are dear to your servants; her very dust moves them to pity.
The nations will fear the name of the Lord, all the kings of the earth will revere your glory.
For the Lord will rebuild Zion and appear in his glory.
He will respond to the prayer of the destitute; he will not despise their plea.

Let this be written for a future generation, that a people not yet created may praise the Lord:
"The Lord looked down from his sanctuary on high, from heaven he viewed the earth,
to hear the groans of the prisoners and release those condemned to death."
So the name of the Lord will be declared in Zion and his praise in Jerusalem
when the peoples and the kingdoms assemble to worship the Lord.

In the course of my life he broke my strength; he cut short my days.
So I said: "Do not take me away, O my God, in the midst of my days; your years go on through all generations.
In the beginning you laid the foundations of the earth, and the heavens are the work of your hands.
They will perish, but you remain; the will all wear out like a garment. Like clothing you will change them and they will be discarded.
But you remain the same, and your years will never end.
The children of your servants will live in your presence; their descendants will be established before you."

Thank you God for including me in the people who praise You. Thank you for writing me a love letter long ago so that I can know what it is to live in your presence. You are a compassionate, responsive God. I love being Your child.

Forget Not All His Benefits

For as high as the heavens are above the earth, so great is his love for those who fear him; as far as the east is from the west, so far has he removed our transgressions from us.

Praise the Lord, O my soul; all my inmost being, praise his holy name.
Praise the Lord, O my soul, and forget not all his benefits.

He forgives all my sins and heals all my diseases; he redeems my life from the pit and crowns me with love and compassion.
He satisfies my desires with good things, so that my youth is renewed like the eagle's.
The Lord works righteousness and justice for all the oppressed.
He made known his ways to Moses, his deeds to the people of Israel:
The Lord is compassionate and gracious, slow to anger, abounding in love.
He will not always accuse, nor will he harbor his anger forever; he does not treat us as our sins deserve or repay us according to our iniquities.
For as high as the heavens are above the earth, so great is his love for those who fear him; as far as the east is from the west, so far has he removed our transgressions from us.
As a father has compassion on his children, so the Lord has compassion on those who fear him.

When my life is in the pit, You remind me that I'm a child of the King. The pit of my sin and sickness gives You an opportunity to forgive me and to heal. When I am tired and depressed, You see it as an opportunity to reveal Your love in a personal way. You make me feel young and hopeful again. You work the disappointments into something good, so that my deeper desires are satisfied.

"Because he loves me ",
says the Lord," I will rescue him, I will
protect him, for he acknowledges
my name. "

From Everlasting to Everlasting the Lord's Love Is

As for man, his days are like grass, he flourishes like a flower of the field.
Praise the Lord, all his works everywhere in his dominion.

Praise the Lord, O my soul.

For he knows how we are formed, he remembers that we are dust.
As for man, his days are like grass, he flourishes like a flower of the field; the wind blows over it and it is gone, and its place remembers it no more.
But from everlasting to everlasting the Lord's love is with those who fear him, and his righteousness with their children's children– with those who keep his covenant and remember to obey his precepts.

The Lord has established his throne in heaven, and his kingdom rules over all.

Praise the Lord, you his angels, you mighty ones who do his bidding, who obey his word.
Praise the Lord, all his heavenly hosts, you his servants who do his will.
Praise the Lord, all his works everywhere in his dominion.

Praise the Lord, O my soul.

We are so fragile; our earthly lives so temporary. Isn't it all the more wonderful that the Lord of all creation loves and gives himself for us? When we praise him for this, we establish his kingdom bit by bit on earth.

Psalm 104

He Makes the Clouds His Chariot

They give water to all the beasts of the field; the wild donkeys quench their thirst.

Praise the Lord, O my soul.

O Lord my God, you are very great; you are clothed with splendor and majesty.
He wraps himself in light as with a garment; he stretches out the heavens like a tent and lays the beams of his upper chambers on their waters. He makes the clouds his chariot and rides on the wings of the wind.
He makes winds his messengers, flames of fire his servants.

He set the earth on its foundations; it can never be moved.
You covered it with the deep as with a garment; the waters stood above the mountains.
But at your rebuke the waters fled, at the sound of your thunder they took to flight; they flowed over the mountains, they went down into the valleys, to the place you assigned for them.
You set a boundary they cannot cross; never again will they cover the earth.

He makes springs pour water into the ravines; it flows between the mountains.
They give water to all the beasts of the field; the wild donkeys quench their thirst.
The birds of the air nest by the waters; they sing among the branches.

You, Lord, are clothed with light. Your earth is clothed with the seas and oceans. And those things are the center of life for mankind. It is good for us to meditate on Your purpose and plan in creation.

The Earth Is Satisfied

He waters the mountains from his upper chambers; the earth is satisfied by the fruit of his work.

He waters the mountains from his upper chambers; the earth is satisfied by the fruit of his work.
He makes grass grow for the cattle, and plants for man to cultivate– bringing forth food from the earth: wine that gladdens the heart of man, oil to make his face shine, and bread that sustains his heart.
The trees of the Lord are well watered, the cedars of Lebanon that he planted.
There the birds make their nests; the stork has its home in the pine trees.
The high mountains belong to the wild goats; the crags are a refuge for the coneys.

The moon marks off the seasons, and the sun knows when to go down.
You bring darkness, it becomes night, and all the beasts of the forest prowl.
The lions roar for their prey and seek their food from God.
The sun rises, and they steal away; they return and lie down in their dens.
Then man goes out to his work, to his labor until evening.

You have worked hard creating the earth. You take pleasure in the pleasure of Your creatures. Thank you, Lord for making me with the ability to be creative and to enjoy it. I'm a student in Your school of design.

May the Lord Rejoice in His Works

May the glory of the Lord endure forever; may the Lord rejoice in his works.
He looks at the earth, and it trembles; he touches the mountains, and they smoke.
I will sing to the Lord all my life; I will sing praise to my God as long as I live.

How many are your works, O Lord! In wisdom you made them all; the earth is full of your creatures.
There is the sea, vast and spacious, teeming with creatures beyond number– living things both large and small.
There the ships go to and fro, and the leviathan, which you formed to frolic there.

These all look to you to give them their food at the proper time.
When you give it to them, they gather it up; when you open your hand, they are satisfied with good things.
When you hide your face, they are terrified; when you take away their breath, they die and return to the dust.
When you send your Spirit, they are created, and you renew the face of the earth.

May the glory of the Lord endure forever; may the Lord rejoice in his works.
He looks at the earth, and it trembles; he touches the mountains, and they smoke.

I will sing to the Lord all my life; I will sing praise to my God as long as I live.
May my meditation be pleasing to him, as I rejoice in the Lord.
But may sinners vanish from the earth and the wicked be no more.

Praise the Lord, O my soul.

Praise the Lord.

We are humbled, God, by the vast number and variety of living things You have created, by the way You use colour, design and function. We are numbered among Your creatures and yet we are more. We are Your people, the apple of Your eye, and someday we will be gathered to You as Your bride. Praise you, God.

Psalm 105

Tell of All His Wonderful Acts

Sing to him, sing praise to him; tell of all his wonderful acts. Glory in his holy name; let the hearts of those who seek the Lord rejoice.

Give thanks to the Lord, call on his name; make known among the nations what he has done.
Sing to him, sing praise to him; tell of all his wonderful acts.
Glory in his holy name; let the hearts of those who seek the Lord rejoice.
Look to the Lord and his strength; seek his face always.
Remember the wonders he has done, his miracles, and the judgments he pronounced, O descendants of Abraham his servant, O sons of Jacob, his chosen ones.

He is the Lord our God; his judgments are in all the earth.
He remembers his covenant forever, the word he commanded, for a thousand generations, the covenant he made with Abraham, the oath he swore to Isaac.
He confirmed it to Jacob as a decree, to Israel as an everlasting covenant:
"To you I will give the land of Canaan as the portion you will inherit."

When they were but few in number, few indeed, and strangers in it, they wandered from nation to nation, from one kingdom to another.
He allowed no one to oppress them; for their sake he rebuked kings: "Do not touch my anointed ones; do my prophets no harm."

He called down famine on the land and destroyed all their supplies of food; and he sent a man before them– Joseph, sold as a slave.
They bruised his feet with shackles, his neck was put in irons, till what he foretold came to pass, till the word of the Lord proved him true.
The king sent and released him, the ruler of peoples set him free.
He made him master of his household, ruler over all he possessed, to discipline his princes as he pleased and teach his elders wisdom.

We have a message to pass on to our neighbours, our cities, our world. We have a heritage to live out and to proclaim to those being re-born. We are children of a Kingdom to be established on earth. We are in process, and part of his great whole.

Then Israel Entered Egypt

The Lord made his people very fruitful...

Then Israel entered Egypt; Jacob lived as an alien in the land of Ham.
The Lord made his people very fruitful; he made them too numerous for their foes, whose hearts he turned to hate his people, to conspire against his servants.
He sent Moses his servant, and Aaron, whom he had chosen.
They performed his miraculous signs among them, his wonders in the land of Ham.
He sent darkness and made the land dark – for had they not rebelled against his words?
He turned their waters into blood, causing their fish to die.
Their land teemed with frogs, which went up into the bedrooms of their rulers.
He spoke, and there came swarms of flies, and gnats throughout their country.
He turned their rain into hail, with lightning throughout their land; he struck down their vines and fig trees and shattered the trees of their country.
He spoke, and the locusts came, grasshoppers without number; they ate up every green thing in their land, ate up the produce of their soil.
Then he struck down all the firstborn in their land, the firstfruits of all their manhood.

In the Egypts of my life, Lord, teach me that even there You will cause me to increase and abound. And when the time is right, You will glorify Yourself in the midst of my situation.

He Remembered His Holy Promise

He spread out a cloud as a covering, and a fire to give light at night.
They asked, and he brought them quail and satisfied them with the bread of heaven.
He opened the rock, and water gushed out; like a river it flowed in the desert.
For he remembered his holy promise given to his servant Abraham.

He brought out Israel, laden with silver and gold, and from among their tribes no one faltered.
Egypt was glad when they left, because dread of Israel had fallen on them.
He spread out a cloud as a covering, and a fire to give light at night.
They asked, and he brought them quail and satisfied them with the bread of heaven.
He opened the rock, and water gushed out; like a river it flowed in the desert.
For he remembered his holy promise given to his servant Abraham.
He brought out his people with rejoicing, his chosen ones with shouts of joy; he gave them the lands of the nations, and they fell heir to what others had toiled for– that they might keep his precepts and observe his laws.

Praise the Lord.

"They fell heir to what others had toiled for..." Why did the Lord allow them prosperity and joy? His purpose was that they might keep his precepts and observe his laws. His goodness is meant to draw us to repentance. He wants us to live out his word in our daily lives, a demonstration to the world of himself.

Praise the Lord, O my soul;
all my inmost being, praise His holy name.
Praise the Lord, O my soul, and
forget not all His benefits.

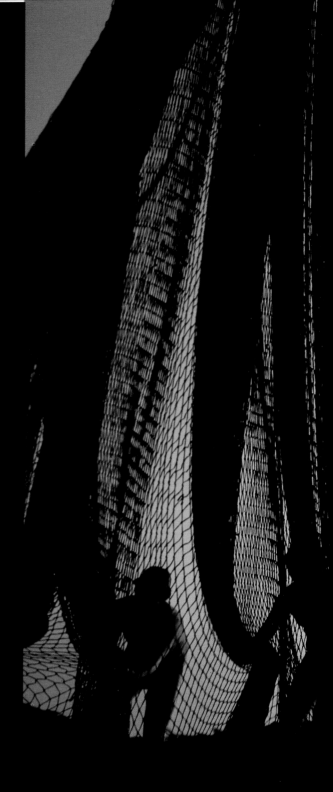

Psalm 106

He Saved Them For His Name's Sake

He rebuked the Red Sea, and it dried up; he led them through the depths as through a desert.

Praise the Lord.

Give thanks to the Lord, for he is good; his love endures forever.
Who can proclaim the mighty acts of the Lord or fully declare his praise?
Blessed are they who maintain justice, who constantly do what is right.
Remember me, O Lord, when you show favor to your people, come to my aid when you save them, that I may enjoy the prosperity of your chosen ones, that I may share in the joy of your nation and join your inheritance in giving praise.

We have sinned, even as our fathers did; we have done wrong and acted wickedly.
When our fathers were in Egypt, they gave no thought to your miracles; they did not remember your many kindnesses, and they rebelled by the sea, the Red Sea.
Yet he saved them for his name's sake, to make his mighty power known.
He rebuked the Red Sea, and it dried up; he led them through the depths as through a desert.
He saved them from the hand of the foe; from the hand of the enemy he redeemed them.
The waters covered their adversaries; not one of them survived.
Then they believed his promises and sang his praise.

But they soon forgot what he had done and did not wait for his counsel.
In the desert they gave in to their craving; in the wasteland they put God to the test.
So he gave them what they asked for, but sent a wasting disease upon them.

In the camp they grew envious of Moses and of Aaron, who was consecrated to the Lord.
The earth opened up and swallowed Dathan; it buried the company of Abiram.
Fire blazed among their followers; a flame consumed the wicked.

I forget so quickly what You have done for me. Fears, longings, envies return so easily. And yet, I have the gift of Your Holy Spirit as the Israelites did not, to fill and refresh my heart. Teach me to continually yield to him bringing You glory and praise.

They Despised the Pleasant Land

They forgot the God who saved them, who had done great things in Egypt, miracles in the land of Ham and awesome deeds by the Red Sea.

At Horeb they made a calf and worshiped an idol cast from metal.
They exchanged their Glory for an image of a bull, which eats grass.
They forgot the God who saved them, who had done great things in Egypt, miracles in the land of Ham and awesome deeds by the Red Sea.
So he said he would destroy them– had not Moses, his chosen one, stood in the breach before him to keep his wrath from destroying them.

Then they despised the pleasant land; they did not believe his promise.
They grumbled in their tents and did not obey the Lord.
So he swore to them with uplifted hand that he would make them fall in the desert, make their descendants fall among the nations and scatter them throughout the lands.

They yoked themselves to the Baal of Peor and ate sacrifices offered to lifeless gods; they provoked the Lord to anger by their wicked deeds, and a plague broke out among them.
But Phinehas stood up and intervened, and the plague was checked.
This was credited to him as righteousness for endless generations to come.

By the waters of Meribah they angered the Lord, and trouble came to Moses because of them; for they rebelled against the Spirit of God, and rash words came from Moses' lips.

Lord, I sense You want to do a deeper work in me than I can see in the ups and downs of my daily life. You need to prune and groom for greater things. I open myself to You. My greatest dread is that You may leave me unfinished because of my stubbornness and lukewarm heart. Dig deeper, Lord.

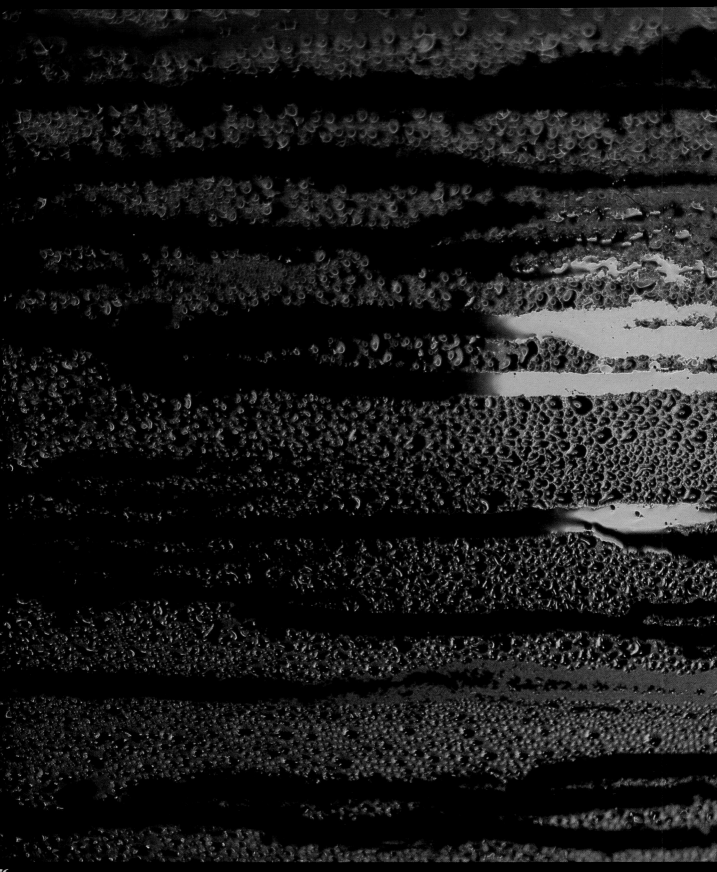

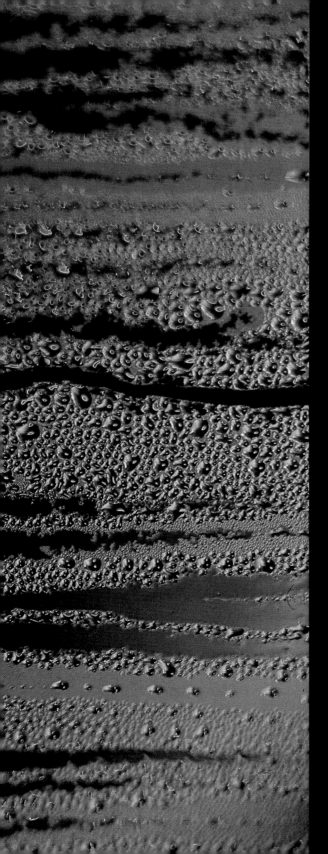

Psalm 106

Let All the People Say, "Amen!"

But he took note of their distress when he heard their cry; for their sake he remembered his covenant and out of his great love he relented.

They did not destroy the peoples as the Lord had commanded them, but they mingled with the nations and adopted their customs.
They worshiped their idols, which became a snare to them.
They sacrificed their sons and their daughters to demons.
They shed innocent blood, the blood of their sons and daughters, whom they sacrificed to the idols of Canaan, and the land was desecrated by their blood.
They defiled themselves by what they did; by their deeds they prostituted themselves.

Therefore the Lord was angry with his people and abhorred his inheritance.
He handed them over to the nations, and their foes ruled over them.
Their enemies oppressed them and subjected them to their power.
Many times he delivered them, but they were bent on rebellion and they wasted away in their sin.

But he took note of their distress when he heard their cry; for their sake he remembered his covenant and out of his great love he relented.
He caused them to be pitied by all who held them captive.

Save us, O Lord our God, and gather us from the nations, that we may give thanks to your holy name and glory in your praise.

Praise be to the Lord, the God of Israel, from everlasting to everlasting. Let all the people say, "Amen!"

Praise the Lord.

Father, thank you for showing us how patient and forgiving Your love really is, and how far Your mercy reaches down. The last great outpouring of Yourself came when You gave us Jesus and allowed his blood to be shed for our sin.

*For as high as the heavens are
above the earth, so great is His love for
those who fear him; as far as the east is from the
west, so far has He removed our
transgressions from us.*

*Praise be to the Lord, the God of Israel,
from everlasting to everlasting. Let all
the people say, "Amen!"*